D1460152

Rhinoceros Beetles as Pets and Hobby

Complete Owner's Guide

Facts, lifespan, habitat, diet, care, breeding, larvae, where to buy all included. Hercules beetle covered.

Table of Contents

Acknowledgment

Writing this book has been a challenge and a pleasure, all thanks to my lovely wife. She has always supported me in my creative endeavors and even accepts my love for unique (she would call them strange) pets.

I would also like to thank my dear friend Daniel for letting me talk his ear off about my love for rhinoceros beetles. You were always a great sounding board as I wrote this book!

Introduction

With its large size and massive horn, the rhinoceros beetle might seem a bit odd. Its unique appearance, as well as its remarkable strength sets it apart from other insects and peaks the interest of those who like to keep and care for unconventional animals.

Though an insect might not be the first thing you'd think of as a pet or a hobby, the rhinoceros beetle has become quite popular in the pet industry. These beetles are safe to handle, easy to keep, and they are relatively clean.

If you're looking for an intriguing new hobby or a pet that is easy to care for and entertaining to keep, think outside the box. The rhinoceros beetles may not be the traditional animals to keep, but they are amazing in their own way. In this book, you'll learn all you need to know about the rhinoceros beetles, as well as how to care for them and breed them.

Although technically not part of the rhinoceros beetle family, I included into this book separate chapters featuring the stag beetle and the Goliath beetle. This is because they are popularly grouped together due to their impressive size and exotic feel. Think of these chapters as bonus chapters. My hope in including them into the book is to help you get an even better overall perspective on the rhino beetle as such.

So, if you're ready to get started, let me introduce you to the rhinoceros beetle!

Chapter 1: Introducing the Rhinoceros Beetle

What is the first thing that comes to mind when you think of the strongest animals in the world? Unless you are a beetle fan already, you'd probably think of the elephant that can lift up to 80 stones (500 kg) or more with its trunk. Yes, when we consider the sheer weight an animal can lift, the elephant would probably be the strongest of all. The same goes for the gorilla that can carry more than ten times its bodyweight. You might even remember the leafcutter ant that can carry up to 50 times its bodyweight. If you did remember the leafcutter ant, then you are on the right track because the strongest animals on the planet are some of the smallest ones.

The fact is, that although big mammals such as the elephant or the gorilla certainly do have impressive strength, they don't even come close to the weightlifting talent of the beetles. You may be surprised to learn that rhino beetles can carry more than 100 times their own bodyweight which puts them into the category of the proportionally strongest animals in the whole world.

But what exactly is the rhinoceros beetle and what else makes it unique from other insects? In this chapter, you'll learn the basics about rhinoceros beetles including some surprising facts. You'll also learn the details of the rhinoceros beetle life cycle.

1. What is the Rhinoceros Beetle?

The name "rhinoceros beetle" applies to a group of beetles belonging to the Dynastinae subfamily which, in turn, is part of the big Scarabaeidae family – the scarab beetle family. They are part of the order Coleoptera and class Insecta. There are more than 300 individual species of rhinoceros beetle that have been identified and described thus far.

The rhinoceros beetle is known for several things that make it unique in its own right – its size, its extraordinary shape, and its strength. Their size varies from one species to another but rhinoceros beetles typically grow larger than 6 inches (15cm) in length.

Given its name, you can probably picture what the rhinoceros beetle looks like without having ever seen one. These insects have the traditional oblong beetle shape in a body that is covered by a thick exoskeleton. Like all insects, they do not have bones. They wear their skeleton on the outside of their body for protection against predators. Their large size also helps protect them against predators that might prefer smaller prey.

As you have probably guessed, rhinoceros beetles get their name from the large horn they carry on their heads. These beetles actually have two horns – a large horn that protrudes from the top of the head and a second horn that projects from the center of the thorax. Both horns are slightly forked on the ends and the beetle is capable of pinching with them by moving its head.

2. Surprising Rhinoceros Beetle Facts

Its size, appearance and strength are by far two of the most interesting things about the rhino beetle but there is so much more. Here are some surprising facts about rhinoceros beetles:

A. They are nocturnal.
B. They can produce a hissing noise.
C. Their larval stage is very long.
D. They are capable of flying.
E. The males sometimes battle each other.
F. They make great pets.

A. Rhinoceros Beetles Are Nocturnal

Combined with their impressive size and formidable appearance, their nocturnal habits help protect the rhinoceros beetle from predators. These beetles can typically be found in vegetation or under logs during the day where they stay hidden from the eyes of a predator. At night, however, they come out to forage for food, looking for fruit, sap, and nectar to feed on. Their nocturnal lifestyle is part of the reason why some of the rhino beetles are so notoriously difficult to spot in the wild.

B. Rhinoceros Beetles Can Produce a Hissing Sound

Rhinoceros beetles are able to produce a hissing noise that can help scare predators away. The beetle produces a loud hissing squeak by rubbing its abdomen against the ends of its wing covers. Rhinoceros beetles tend to make this sound when they are disturbed and feel threatened. It can sound scary or, at least, odd if you've never heard a hissing sound coming from a beetle, but it's really nothing more than a bluff.

C. The Larval Stage Is Very Long

Rhinoceros beetles have a very long larval stage. More specifically, their larval stage can last several years. During this stage, the larvae feed on rotting wood and compost until they develop into pupae and then into adult beetles. Developing larvae consume surprisingly large amounts of food as they grow. Much more so than an adult beetle.

D. Rhinoceros Beetles Are Capable of Flight

The presence of wings in beetles does not automatically mean that they are able to fly. Some species cannot fly at all, while others can only do so within a certain temperature range. When you see a rhinoceros beetle and take in its massive size, you might assume that flying would be impossible. In reality, however, these beetles fly just as well as any other. They are actually very good at flying. Rumor has it that its ability to fly, despite its weight, makes it a hot candidate for future aircraft design.

Because these beetles are nocturnal, you may find them flying around lights at night. In cooler climates, they tend to be most active during the summer months but, in warmer areas, they can be seen flying around street lights all year round.

E. Male Rhinoceros Beetles Battle Each Other

While many animals exhibit ornate bodily structures only to attract a mate, the rhinoceros beetle's horns are designed to be used as a battle tool. They can be used to grab or even throw an opposing beetle in a fight for a female's attention. Every species of rhinoceros beetle has a slightly different horn and they each have their own unique fighting style as well.

Though many people keep rhinoceros beetles as pets or as a hobby, there is a subset of owners who keep them for an entirely different reason – battle. The popularity of rhinoceros beetle fighting has remained steadfast. In fact, it has developed into a gambling sport in some parts of the world.

When it comes to the mechanics of rhinoceros beetle fighting, the guidelines are simple. All that is needed is a pair of male beetles and a sturdy log to place them on. In beetle battles, each insect owner places his beetle on one end of the log and then they watch as the insects lock horns and attempt to throw each other off. Whichever beetle remains at the end of the match is declared the winner.

To some people, rhinoceros beetle battles are in the same category as other types of animal fighting like bull baiting or dog fighting. To others, however, it is harmless fun. Luckily for those whose heart goes to the fighting rhino beetles, the loser's hard exoskeleton protects him from harm should he fall off the log.

F. Rhinoceros Beetles Make Great Pets

Though a beetle might not be your first choice when it comes to picking a new pet, they are a fascinating animal to keep and care for. Rhinoceros beetles are, clearly, nothing like cats, dogs, and other traditional pets, especially when it comes to bonding and their responsiveness to a human being. This is the reason why some people consider owning a beetle a hobby, rather than having a pet. In addition, rhinoceros beetles are relatively clean and easy to care for.

Because they are completely harmless to humans and require relatively little time to care, they make great pets for children!

Chapter 2: Understanding the Rhinoceros Beetle

Now that you have a general understanding of what the rhinoceros beetle is, you may be curious to know exactly how these animals came to be. It may or may not shock you to learn that beetles like the rhinoceros beetle have existed for millions of years on Earth and many of the oldest species found in fossil form are strikingly similar to the modern species that exist today.

In this chapter, you'll learn more about the history of keeping rhinoceros beetles as pets. You'll also receive an overview of the history of the rhinoceros beetle and a foray into its evolution.

1. History of the Rhinoceros Beetle as a Pet

Throughout history, beetles have maintained a prominent place as an object of human fascination. In ancient Egypt, scarab beetles were kept as pets and used as fighting insects. They were also part of the Egyptian folklore and symbolism where the scarab beetle represented, among other things, a new life since it was associated with one of the Egyptian deities. A lot of amulets from Ancient Egypt hold the form of a scarab beetle. In fact, many ancient artifacts depict precisely this beetle. Even today, the scarab beetle is still popular as a good luck charm design.

Beetles are extremely popular in the Japanese culture. Keeping them as pets is far from unusual. Even outside one's home, establishments such as beetle petting zoos allow children, as well as adults, to interact with beetles, observe them and play with them. Convenience stores across Japan sell rhinoceros beetles at a price ranging from 500 to 1000 yen which equals roughly 5 to 10 U.S. dollars. Japanese department stores often contain insect corners within pet sections, where live beetles are sold as pets along with the relevant equipment, literature and supplies.

The beetle fascination of some Asian countries (such as Japan) is sometimes referred to as "beetle mania", but this trend is slowly but surely spreading across the world. It is becoming increasingly popular these days to keep many different kinds of insects as pets including roaches, moths, centipedes, and praying mantises.

Owning insects has become more than just a fleeting interest, it has become a trend. Having said that, it is by no means a new practice. People have been keeping insects as pets for thousands of years. Apart from Japan, children collected crickets in ancient China, keeping them as pets and organizing fights with other children. The strongest cricket was declared the winner and was then used to breed an entirely new generation of fighting crickets. Other insects, primarily production insects like silkworms and silk moths, were also kept in China and bred to produce silk.

Today, people keep insects as pets for a variety of different reasons. For one thing, they are often easier to keep than traditional pets. They also take up less space. A lot of insect owners keep insects as pets for their unique colors, shapes, and interesting behavior.

There is a certain degree of challenge involved in raising insects, especially rhinoceros beetles. The beetles themselves may only live for a few months but it can take years to cultivate them from egg to larva to pupa to adult.

Then, of course, some people find passion in breeding beetles. Hobbyists with this particular passion are known to compete with each other trying to breed the biggest beetle exemplar possible.

Rhinoceros beetles are not the only insect that is popular as a pet today. The most common insect pets include:

- Walking sticks
- Cockroaches
- Praying mantises
- Ants
- Centipedes

- Millipedes
- Scorpions
- Tarantulas
- Butterflies/moths
- Beetles

The good news is that keeping and breeding beetles contributes to the body of knowledge we have about beetles overall. Believe it or not, there is still so much we don't know about them! Some species rarely even come into contact with humans as they spend their lives in the soil, hidden under the logs, rocks and leaves. In a way, rhino beetles and stag beetles are still a mystery – one that breeders and hobbyist continue to unveil. Rearing them in captivity enables us to fill in the gaps that exist when it comes to the life of these amazing, giant beetles.

Keep in mind that not all beetles are necessarily legal to keep as pets in your own country and that you always need to find out the legalities of owning a beetle before procuring one. Stag beetles and Goliath beetles are a good example. We will talk more about the legalities in a later chapter. For now, let's look at the evolution of the rhino beetle.

2. Evolution of the Rhinoceros Beetle

When you think about some of the oldest animals on Earth – animals that have remained relatively unchanged by the hands of evolution – you might think of various sea creatures like the horseshoe crab or the coelacanth. What you may not realize, however, is that some of the animals that have been on the Earth the longest are the ones you see every day – insects.

According to scientific research, the evolutionary lineage of most of the beetle species that exist today was originally developed during the Jurassic period. That makes them more than 145 million years old. Many of the oldest insect specimens collected by scientists are encased in amber. The fact that the insects were encased in this substance suggests that they lived on or under the bark of these trees. To date, more than 60 different beetle families have been found preserved in amber and many of them still occur today.

Though various insects have undergone differing degrees of evolutionary change over the years, most of the fossil beetles that were collected from the Quaternary period (from 2.6 million to present) are nearly identical to the beetles that exist today.

As you now know, the modern rhinoceros beetle belongs to the Dynastinae which is a subfamily of Scarabaeidae, the scarab beetle family. This family falls into the suborder Polyphaga of the order Coleoptera in the class Insecta.

The Insecta class contains myriad families and genera, but there are certain characteristics all insects share. They have a chitinous exoskeleton, a three-part body, three pairs of jointed legs, compound eyes, and a single pair of antennae.

The estimated number of insect species that currently exist is somewhere between 6 and 10 million. In terms of sheer quantity, the Earth is populated by about a quintillion of insects! Part of the reason behind this impressive quantity is that insects are extremely adaptable and they exist in all types of climate worldwide, even in Antarctica.

The order Coleoptera is the order to which beetles belong. There are an estimated 400,000 species in the Coleoptera order which makes it the largest of all taxonomical orders. In fact, the order Coleoptera alone accounts for 40% of all insects that have been described to this day and 25% of all animal life forms on Earth! In other words, every fourth animal species is a beetle. Bear in mind that this number (400,000) depicts just the number of documented and described beetles. New species of beetles still get discovered on a relatively frequent basis. This is why the famous British geneticist J.B.S. Haldane stated that god must have "an inordinate fondness for beetles" when he was asked what his studies of nature revealed about god.

Beetles come in all shapes and sizes. They are huge and they are tiny, some of them are plain, some of them make you gasp when you spot their impressive colors. One way or another, they interact with the ecosystem in several important ways.

Many beetles feed on plants and fungi, breaking down organic debris and recycling dead matter back into the ecosystem. Beetles also pollinate different species of plants and help maintain the balance in plant species by being herbivorous. Some of them eat invertebrates and insect pests that harm agricultural crops, while others fulfill the role of much needed scavengers.

Generally speaking, the anatomy of the beetle is very similar across all genera and species despite the huge quantity of them. Beetles have an external skeleton (almost like a shell), as opposed to the internal skeleton we can observe in humans. This skeleton is called *exoskeleton* and is very hard. The wing cases that cover the hind part of the body and protect the wings are also very hard. They are called *elytra* and are not used for flying as such. However, they do need to be raised in order for the beetle to fly.

Beetles are Endopterygota, that means insects that undergo a complete metamorphosis that includes a series of abrupt changes to their bodily structure between the time they hatch from eggs and progress from the pupal stage into adulthood. Some beetles even exhibit sexual dimorphism - anatomical differences between the sexes. This is certainly the case when it comes to rhino beetles. The differences between a male and female beetle are easily noticeable.

The rhinoceros beetle is a member of the Scarabaeidae family which consists of more than 30,000 species. These beetles are stout-bodied and range from the size of a pinhead to over six inches (16cm) in length. Scarab beetles have broad front legs that many species use for digging and clubbed antennae that can be compressed into a ball or fanned out to detect odors.

In the larval stage, beetles in the family Scarabaeidae are C-shaped and pale yellow or white in color. As they develop, the larvae typically called grubs, live underground to avoid exposure to sunlight. When they become adults, they are often nocturnal (including rhinoceros beetles).

More than 300 species of rhinoceros beetles belong to the Dynastinae subfamily. They are known for their traditional beetle shape but more so for their large, pointed horns.

To gain a better understanding of the rhinoceros beetle's evolution, scientists studied the different species and their horns to determine whether they were evolutionary beneficial or not. Erin McCullough, a doctoral student at the University of Montana, found that the beetles' horns didn't detract from evolutionary natural selection at all.

In taking a closer look, McCullough found that the horns themselves were largely hollow and dry. This meant that they didn't impair the beetle's ability to fly and they didn't change its center of mass. Because the different horn shapes didn't detract from the species' survival, evolutionary diversity was allowed to continue unfettered for thousands of years.

The drivers for this level of diversity are still poorly understood, but it is certainly worth noticing how the different horn shapes reflect the unique structural adaptations and different fighting styles for which each species of rhinoceros beetle is known.

3. The Rhinoceros Beetle Life Cycle

All insects go through a specific life cycle through which they develop from eggs into adults. The number of stages in the life cycle, as well as the length of time it takes to progress through them, varies from one family of insect to another (and in some cases, from one species to another).

The life cycle of rhinoceros beetles has four stages. In the first stage, the female beetle lays an average of 50 eggs. The eggs are very small, ovular in shape, and white or yellow in color. She will typically deposit them on a leaf or inside a rotten log for protection.

After the eggs have been deposited, it usually takes between 3 and 4 weeks for them to hatch. The second stage in the rhino beetle life cycle is the larval stage. This is when the eggs hatch. They hatch into tiny grubs or maggot-like larvae. During this stage, the larvae will consume large amounts of rotten wood and other organic materials to fuel their growth and development.

There are three substages of the larval stage in which the larvae molt to allow for new growth - L1, L2, and L3.

The larval stage for rhinoceros beetles is remarkably long compared to that of many other insects. Though the length may vary from one species to another, the rhino beetle's larval stage can take a year or more. After the larvae exit the third substage (L3), they'll start to darken in color and they'll develop wrinkles. These wrinkles are the signs that the larvae are entering the pupal stage.

Once the larvae develop into pupae, they will dig themselves a hole in the soil where they will complete their final molt. During this stage, the pupae do not need any food or special care. You simply have to wait for an adult rhinoceros beetle to emerge.

As adults, the beetles will go through a short resting period before they begin breeding again. The total lifespan of the adult rhinoceros beetle is usually 3 to 6 months, though the entire life cycle may last as long as 2 or 3 years in captivity.

4. Types of Rhinoceros Beetles

When it comes to the different species of rhinoceros beetle, there are more than 300 that have already been discovered but there could be more. Rhino beetles that are most commonly bred and kept in captivity as pets or hobby belong to the following genera:

- *Allomyrina*
- *Chalcosoma*
- *Dynastes*
- *Eupatorus*
- *Megasoma*
- *Xylotrupes*

Within these six genera are many different species. For example, the popular Hercules beetle belongs to the *Dynastes* genus. Other popular rhino beetles include the elephant beetle (*Megasoma elephas*), the European rhinoceros beetle (*Oryctes nasicornis*) , and the Japanese rhinoceros beetle (*Allomyrina dichotoma*).

The next chapters will walk you through some of the most popular types of these beetles, including the stag beetle and the Goliath beetle that I added for completion. The two latter ones don't technically belong to the same family as rhino beetles. However, because they are often grouped together by the general public, they are included as special chapters towards the end of the book.

Chapter 3: Hercules Beetles

Known both as the Hercules beetle and the unicorn beetle, this species is easily one of the largest beetles in the world, certainly the largest of the rhinoceros beetles. Found primarily in the jungle of South America, you can also find the Hercules beetle in parts of Central, as well as North America. They are largely nocturnal insects, foraging through leaf litter on the forest floor to find food under the cover of darkness.

Named after one of the greatest heroes of Greek mythology for its remarkable strength, these beetles have two pincer-like horns protruding from their head. The exact size and shape of these horns varies by species, but they have the potential to grow longer than the beetle's body in some species, especially for male beetles. Male beetles use these horns to battle each other for the attention of the female who has no horns but may be larger, if shorter, in body than the male.

The Hercules beetle is an omnivorous species but only because its diet varies from one life stage to another. In its larval form, they subsist primarily on rotting wood and leaf litter. In its adult form, they eat tree sap and fruit. They will, however, eat the occasional insect which is what makes them omnivorous. In captivity, they feed mostly on fruit.

In its adult form, the Hercules beetle grows about 2 to 3.5 inches (5 to 8.75cm) long and 1 to 1.65 inches (2.5 to 4.2cm) wide. Males may measure as much as 6.8 inches (17cm) when you factor in the length of their horn.

Male Hercules beetles have black bodies except for the elytra, or forewings, which are olive-green in color and may exhibit black spots. Females not only have no horn, but they exhibit puncture elytra that are almost entirely black.

As is true for most rhinoceros beetles, little is known about their life cycle in the wild. In captivity, however, Hercules beetles take 2 to 3 years to progress from an egg to an adult beetle. Mating usually occurs during the rainy season in the wild and females normally go through a gestation period of about 30 days before depositing their eggs. The eggs hatch within 3 to 4 weeks upon which they enter the larval stage.

The larval stage alone can last up to 2 years with the larvae growing up to 4.5 inches (11cm) long and weighing over 3.5 ounces (100g). The larval stage consists of three substages, or instars. The first lasts 50 days, the second 56 days, and the third 450 days. After the larval stage, these beetles become pupae. They dig into the ground and develop over the course of 32 days into adult beetles. Once they reach adulthood, Hercules beetles have an average lifespan of 3 to 6 months, although in captivity they may live longer.

There are currently seven species of Hercules beetle that have been identified. They are listed below:

- *Dynastes grantii*
- *Dynastes hercules*
- *Dynastes hyllus*
- *Dynastes maya*
- *Dynastes neptunus*
- *Dynastes satanas*
- *Dynastes tityus*

In addition to their large horns, another thing Hercules beetles are known for, is their ability to make a huffing noise. When they feel threatened, they rub their abdomen against their elytra to make a loud sound to deter predators.

When it comes to communication within their own species, they use a combination of chemoreception, sight, and mechanical perception.

1. Species of Hercules Beetles

As you've already learned, there are seven different species of Hercules beetle. The Eastern Hercules beetle (*Dynastes tityus*) is one of the most commonly known species, aside from *Dynastes hercules*, of course. The Eastern Hercules beetle is found in the Eastern United States ranging from New York through Illinois and Indiana down to Florida and Texas.

Eastern Hercules beetles range in size from 0.8 to 1.1 inches (20 to 27mm) wide and from 1.6 to 2.4 inches (40 to 60mm) long, including the length of the horn that projects from the thorax of male beetles.

Given the size of this beetle and the size of its horn, this species is one of the longest and heaviest beetles in the entire United States. They use their horns to battle other males in rivalry for a mate and the size of the horn may vary from one specimen to another depending on the availability of food when the beetle was growing.

Eastern Hercules beetles are usually tan, gray, or green in color with a mottled black pattern on the elytra. Each specimen has its own pattern of spots and their color may change according to the level of moisture in the habitat in which they are found. Beetles living in the soil or in rotten wood tend to be darker in color.

The mating process for Eastern Hercules beetles is very long – it lasts up to 50 minutes. After mating, the eggs are typically deposited at the same site. Larvae of this species are very large and C-shaped with white bodies and chewing mouthparts. The larvae feed on decaying wood and develop over the course of 12 to 18 months until they create a pupal cell where they develop into adults. Adult beetles usually emerge in the summer and live for about 3 to 6 months.

The Western Hercules beetle (*Dynastes grantii*) is found in the western part of the United States, typically at higher elevations throughout Arizona and Utah as well as parts of Mexico. These beetles grow 2 to 3.1 inches (5 to 8cm) in length and they typically emerge as adults between August and September. Though the larvae take 2 to 3 years to develop, the adults only live for 2 to 4 months. This species has a tan or light gray color that turns dark, nearly black, when the beetle lives in a moist habitat.

An example of a species of Hercules beetle that is native to South America, is the Satanas beetle (*Dynastes satanas*). This species is native to Bolivia and it is an endangered species due to habitat loss. These beetles grow 2 to 4.5 inches (5 to 11.5cm) in males and 1.2 to 2.2 inches (3 to 5.5cm) in females. Males also have a single large horn growing out of the pronotum and are dark in color with a reddish pubescence on the underside. This species has a biennial life cycle with eggs hatching about 2 months after being deposited and larvae taking 1.5 to 2 years to develop.

2. Summary of Hercules Beetle Facts

Common Name: Hercules beetle, unicorn beetle

Scientific Name: *Dynastes*

Habitat: North America, Central America, South America

Size: 2 to 3.5 inches (5 to 8.5cm), up to 6.8 inches (17.5cm) long with horn

Lifespan: 2 to 3 years total; 3 to 6 months as adults

Housing: tank or terrarium at least 5x body length

Temperature: 68°F to 78°F (20°C to 26°C)

Humidity: 70%

Chapter 4: Elephant Beetles

The elephant beetle is a type of neotropical rhinoceros beetle native to South America, Central America, as well as Mexico. These beetles are large, black in color, and covered in a fine coating of microscopic hairs which grow particularly thick on the elytra. These hairs often give the body the appearance of having a more yellow-green color. Male elephant beetles have two large horns protruding from the head and a smaller one from the prothorax but the female has no horns.

As a type of rhinoceros beetle, elephant beetles are very large. They grow from 2.75 to 4.75 inches (7 to 12cm) in length. On average, males are two to three times larger than females. Males also differ in their behavior. They have been known to fight other males not only for the right to mate with a female, but over food as well.

Some of the most common bred and kept species of elephant beetles (genus *Megasoma*) are the following ones:

- *Megasoma elephas*
- *Megasoma actaeon*
- *Megasoma punctulatum*

Like other rhinoceros beetles, elephant beetles feed primarily on tree sap in the wild but will eat fruits like bananas and apples in captivity. They will also eat more exotic fruits like pineapple, lychee, and longan, as well as the bark from certain trees. These beetles live in the rainforest and they are primarily nocturnal insects. In their native habitat, they have been hit hard by deforestation which has significantly reduced their mating grounds and thus their population.

Elephant beetles take an average of two to three years to develop from eggs into adults. As soon as the eggs hatch in to larvae, the larvae consume what's left of the egg skin and then immediately start feeding on substrate. The speed of their development is highly dependent on temperature. The best temperature range for larval development is 64°F to 77°F (18°C to 25°C) but you still need to maintain around 70% humidity. One important difference between raising elephant beetle larvae and other rhinoceros beetle larvae is that this species feeds more on decaying leaf litter than on rotting wood.

The average elephant larva completes the first larval substage within 3 to 5 weeks and the second within 6 to 9 weeks. The third substage can take anywhere from 8 to 16 months, throughout which, they may go through several molts. With each molt, the body of the larva changes but the head capsule does not grow. Once the larvae complete the larval stage, they enter pupation. The average female weight at the start of pupation is 2.1 ounces

(60g) and the average male weight is about 3.2 ounces (90g), though they can be as heavy as 4.9 ounces (140g).

Pupating elephant beetles need a lot of space – for about 4 large larvae you'll need a 6 to 8 gallon (25 to 30l) tub or tank. To help the larvae form a strong pupal cell, the tub should be lined with rich soil. Over the next 2 to 3 months, the pupae will develop and they should not be disturbed during this time.

When they finally finish developing into adults, they will then go through a resting period of 4 to 6 weeks during which the exoskeleton will harden. At this point, the temperature should be maintained at 68°F to 77°F (20°C to 25°C) and the humidity as high as possible. After they've emerged, you can give them a week or two of feeding before mating them.

1. Summary of Elephant Beetle Facts

Common Name: elephant beetle

Scientific Name: *Megasoma*

Habitat: South America, Central America, and Mexico

Size: 2.75 to 4.75 inches (7 to 12cm)

Lifespan: 2 to 3 years total; 3 to 6 months as adults

Housing: tank or terrarium at least 5x body length

Temperature: 68°F to 78°F (20°C to 26°C)

Humidity: 70%

Chapter 5: Japanese Rhinoceros Beetles

The Japanese rhinoceros beetle is found throughout Japan as well as Taiwan, eastern China, and the Korean peninsula. These beetles are also known as the Japanese horned beetle or by their Japanese name, *kabutomushi*. There are several subspecies of Japanese rhinoceros beetle that can be found in broad-leaved forests in both tropical and subtropical mountain habitats:

- *Allomyrina dichotoma dichotoma*
- *Allomyrina dichotoma inchachina*
- *Allomyrina dichotoma septentrionalis*
- *Allomyrina dichotoma takarai*
- *Allomyrina dichotoma tunobosonis*
- *Allomyrina dichotoma politus*
- *Allomyrina dichotoma tsuchiyai*
- *Allomyrina dichotoma shizuae*

Like other rhinoceros beetles, the Japanese rhinoceros beetle only lives an average of 4 months as an adult beetle. Most of its life is spent underground. In their native habitat, the adult beetles tend to emerge in late spring and they die between mid-September and early October after they have mated and deposited their eggs.

The adult beetles are very large with dark brown bodies and red or white eyes. Males of the species are generally much larger than females, growing up to 1.5 to 3 inches (4 to 8cm) while females only grow to 1.5 to 2.4 inches (4 to 6cm). Similar to the Hercules beetle, the length of the Japanese rhinoceros beetle's horn can be just as long, or longer than, the body itself. The largest horn is Y-shaped with a smaller forked horn on the thorax.

1. Summary of Japanese Rhinoceros Beetle Facts

Common Name: Japanese rhinoceros beetle

Scientific Name: *Allomyrina dichotoma*

Habitat: Japan, Taiwan, eastern China, Korean peninsula

Size: 1.5 to 3 inches (4 to 8cm)

Lifespan: 2 to 3 years total; 3 to 6 months as adults

Housing: tank or terrarium at least 5x body length

Temperature: 68°F to 78°F (20°C to 26°C)

Humidity: 70%

Chapter 6: Coconut Rhinoceros Beetles

The coconut rhinoceros beetle is a smaller species of rhinoceros beetle that only grows to about 2 inches (5cm) in length – females may be a little smaller. These beetles have dark brown or black bodies with a shiny exoskeleton. Both males and females have horns on the tops of their heads, but the male's horn is larger and can be used to fight off other males when competing for mates or food.

Coconut rhinoceros beetles can be found in the Asian tropics ranging from Pakistan to the Philippines. They have also been introduced in the South Pacific where they are commonly recognized as insect pests which is why they are not allowed to be imported to many countries! These beetles attack coconut and oil palms which is how they got their name. They burrow into the center of the crown, feeding on the sap and cutting through the developing leaves in the process. In fact, the problem became so pronounced that the United Nations established a fund to aid with the eradication of the species from the South Pacific.

The care and breeding of coconut rhinoceros beetles is similar to that of other rhinoceros beetles and is covered in detail in a later chapter. In general, these beetles hatch from eggs after about 8 to 12 days at which point they enter the larval stage. Coconut rhinoceros beetle larvae feed and grow for another 82 to 207 days. After that, they enter the pre-pupal stage. During this stage, the larvae spend 8 to 13 days developing their pupal cell which they then enter for 17 to 22 days before emerging as adults. The adult beetle lives for 4 to 9 months and females lay an average of 50 to 100 eggs in their lifetime.

1. Summary of Coconut Rhinoceros Beetle Facts

Common Name: coconut rhinoceros beetle

Scientific Name: *Oryctes rhinoceros*

Habitat: Asia and South Pacific Islands

Size: about 2 inches (5cm)

Lifespan: 2 to 3 years total; 4 to 9 months as adults

Housing: tank or terrarium at least 5x body length

Temperature: 68°F to 78°F (20°C to 26°C)

Humidity: 70%

Chapter 7: Rhinoceros Beetles as Pets and Hobby

When hearing the word "pet", most people probably wouldn't think of a beetle. Dogs, cats, canaries, turtles or bunnies are the more likely candidates. But what exactly does the word "pet" mean, and why does it have to be limited to traditional pets?

A pet is simply an animal that you keep for your own enjoyment, though everyone's reason for keeping a pet is different. Although a rhinoceros beetle might not be the kind of pet you cuddle with on the couch or take for a walk, they are still brilliant and entertaining. In this chapter, you'll learn the basics about keeping a rhinoceros beetle as a pet or as a hobby including things to know before you buy, pros and cons of keeping them, as well as tips and tricks for caring for and breeding these beetles.

1. What Should You Know Before Getting One?

Before you settle on keeping a rhinoceros beetle, you need to think carefully about whether it is truly the best option for you. Even if you don't expect cuddles from this animal and want to keep it strictly as a hobby, you will be responsible for providing your beetle with a suitable habitat and a healthy diet.

The first question you need to ask yourself before getting a rhinoceros beetle is why do you want one? For the most part, rhinoceros beetles are easy to care for, relatively clean, and they don't cost a lot to keep. Furthermore, they only have a lifespan of 2 to 3 years, including the time they spend developing from an egg into an adult. If you're looking for a low-maintenance pet and a hobby that won't take up a lot of space and consume too much of your time, the rhinoceros beetle might be a good fit.

Another question you should ask yourself is whether you want your children to get along with the beetle, if you have any. The first thing to think about is safety. Could your children be hurt by the beetle or vice versa? One of the greatest things about rhinoceros beetles is the fact that they are completely harmless to humans. Occasionally, some species might be able to pinch with their horns, but even then, their horns can generally do so only weakly. Rhino beetles are substantial in size and protected by a hard exoskeleton, so gentle handling by older children should be no problem. In fact, keeping them could be an excellent way to peak your child's interest in the fascinating world of animals and nature at large.

In addition to considering your personal reasons for choosing a rhino beetle and thinking about your kids, you should also ask yourself whether you can commit to caring for your beetle for the duration of his life. If you plan to become a pet owner (no matter what kind of pet you choose), you should be able to commit to caring for that pet for its entire life.

For a rhinoceros beetle, this might mean caring for an adult for a few months or it might mean raising your beetle from an egg to an adult over the course of two years or more. Either way, make sure you are ready to make the commitment before you buy a rhino beetle.

2. Pros and Cons of Keeping Rhinoceros Beetles

You've thought about and answered some important questions posed in the previous section, but before you make your official decision, take a moment to consider both the pros and cons of keeping rhinoceros beetles.

Pros for keeping rhinoceros beetles

- They are a very unique and attractive looking insect.
- They do not require a large habitat.
- They don't eat a lot of food as adult beetles.
- They are docile and safe to handle.
- They are clean and low-maintenance.
- They are relatively inexpensive to keep.

Cons for keeping rhinoceros beetles

- They require a certain temperature and humidity.
- They have specific dietary requirements.
- They will not form an attachment to their owner.
- They only live for a few months as adults.
- They may be tricky to buy if you're looking for a specific species or variant.

Now that you've considered the pros and cons for keeping rhinoceros beetles, you should have most of the information you need to decide whether this beetle might be for you. The remaining two sections in this chapter will provide you with some practical information about where to buy rhino beetles and how much they cost to keep.

3. Where to Buy Rhinoceros Beetles?

If you think that the rhinoceros beetle might be the right choice for you, your next step is to start looking around for a place to buy one. Before you do, take a moment to consider whether you want to buy a fully developed adult or whether you want to raise your own beetle. If you purchase an adult, you may only get to spend a few months with it. If you raise your beetle from an egg or larva, however, you may get to enjoy two or three years together.

Once you've decided how you want to keep or raise your beetle, start looking around for a place to buy one. If you live in an area where these beetles are native, avoid the temptation to simply go out and find one yourself. Not only might it be illegal to collect and keep wildlife, but it could be more challenging to care for a wild-caught beetle than a captive-bred beetle, especially when it comes to feeding it.

Now, where do you start looking to find adult rhinoceros beetles or rhinoceros beetle larvae for sale?

The easiest way to find rhinoceros beetles for sale is to perform a simple online search. By searching for the specific species you want, you can find several breeders or sellers to choose from. If you're lucky, there will be a brick and mortar pet shop in your area that will make it possible for you to buy one directly. This is an ideal option because you will have the certainty that the species being sold there are legal to buy and keep. However, if you don't find a brick and mortar shop, there are still opportunities to buy your beetle through an online shop.

Once you have a few options, take the time to vet them thoroughly before you make a purchase. Don't rush and see if the breeder is actually knowledgeable about the rhinoceros beetles to ensure that the beetle you buy is properly bred.

You'll also want to ask about shipping methods to make sure your beetle or larvae arrive safely. Most legitimate sellers will have the terms of conditions for dispatching and shipping clearly spelled out on their website. They will also explain what steps they take in order for the beetle to be shipped as ethically and safely as possible. In fact, this is one indicator letting you know that the seller is knowledgeable and cares for these animals.

Please, bear in mind that it is best if you choose the quickest way of delivery as to prevent your beetle from staying in the delivery box longer than necessary. In fact, legit sites won't even give you the option of choosing a slow delivery. Also, once you place your order, track your package and make sure that you don't miss the delivery!

In order to find out if an online beetle vendor is trustworthy, take the time to carefully review their website. The information you want to be on the lookout for can be summarized as the answers to the following questions:

- How long have you been raising and selling beetles?
- Where do you get your beetle eggs and larvae?
- Do you have a license or permit to breed and sell beetles?
- What do you feed your beetles and larvae?
- How do you ship the beetles to ensure that they arrive alive?
- Do you offer any kind of money-back guarantee on shipments?

If you don't find this information by giving the vendor's site a good read, then don't hesitate and contact the seller directly in order to find out what you need. Many sellers are beetle enthusiasts and will be happy to give you the information you are looking for.

If the vendor says that they have a permit or license to breed and sell and you want to be extra cautious, check with the company that issued the permit to ensure that it's valid.

If you don't feel comfortable buying a beetle online, you might be able to find them closer to home by attending a local expo or an event such as a reptile show or maybe even a beetle show. You can find information about pet expos and shows in your local newspaper, your local pet store or online. Try talking to the staff at any local pet stores to see if they have any information for you.

When attending a pet expo or reptile show, take your time looking around and always ask the vendor the questions provided earlier before you buy. Even if you don't find the exact beetle you want at the show, you can make some valuable contacts. Ask around for recommendations on where to find the beetle you want and whether the vendors at the show can connect you directly to a breeder. Buying directly can save you a lot of money on shipping costs and it saves your beetle the stress of shipping. If all else fails, you can order eggs or larvae online and raise them yourself. Don't forget that numerous additional resources are listed at the back of this book.

4. How Much Does It Cost to Keep One?

One final question to consider before you decide for certain whether the rhinoceros beetle is the ideal pet for you is whether you can afford to keep one.

You'll need to purchase a tank, substrate, decorations, and tank equipment on top of the cost of your beetle. Then, you'll need to feed your beetle and care for it in the long run. Here is a quick approximate breakdown of the costs:

Estimated Cost to Keep Rhinoceros Beetles

Upfront Costs

Item	Cost $	Cost €
Tank (ex: 10-gallon (38l) aquarium)	$20	€17
Tank Decorations (ex: wooden branches, wood chips, etc.)	$15 to $25	€13 to €21
Incandescent Light Fixture	$15	€13
Plastic Spray Bottle	< $5	< €4.25
Rhinoceros Beetle (larvae)	$9 to $35	€8 to €30
Rhinoceros Beetle (adult)	$40 to $180	€35 to €150
Subtotal	**$104 to $280**	**€90 to €235**

Monthly Costs

Item	Cost $	Cost €
Substrate (ex: rich potting soil)	$10	€8.50
Food (decayed wood for larvae)	$10	€8.50
Food (fruit for adult beetles)	$10	€8.50
Replacement Light Bulbs	< $5	€4.25
Subtotal	**$35**	**€30**

5. Do You Need a License or Permit?

One final thing you need to consider before bringing home a rhinoceros beetle is the legal side of things. Generally speaking, rhinoceros beetles are not endangered, so it is possible to legally keep and breed them in most countries. Restrictions may exist when it comes to some species. But to be absolutely certain about the species you are planning on bringing home, you always want to check the law before you buy. Especially, if you are not getting your beetle from a reputable local source.

Laws and regulations change constantly and they also differ from one country to another. There are species that might not have been endangered or illegal to keep in the past in your country, but now they are. Or vice versa, some species could have been added to the list of animals that are now allowed to be kept in captivity.

I wish there was an easy way to tell you if it's legal to keep and breed a specific type of beetle in the country where you live. But because of the differences in law between countries, the best I can do for the reader is to offer generic guidelines.

Before we get into legally keeping your beetle, let's consider the question of collecting living animals from the wild. It's always best to buy your beetle from a reputable source. First of all, it may be illegal to collect beetles from the wild in your country (many laws refer to this as "hunting" and "trapping" of animals in the wild, both of which are illegal). Second, when you buy from a reputable seller, chances are much higher that you're not buying a threatened species.

Whether you buy your beetle locally or have it delivered to you from somewhere else, it is ultimately your responsibility to know whether or not the law allows keeping a certain species in captivity or whether there are any restrictions such as needing a permit or a license. For most rhinoceros beetles, this is not the case and keeping them might be fairly straightforward in your country. But just for the sake of having a complete picture, let me mention some issues to consider when keeping beetles as such.

If you are ordering your beetle non-locally, there are two main questions to consider:

1) Can you import a specific species into your country?
2) Can you keep a specific species in captivity?

Many countries have gradually banned certain species of animals from being imported. There are several reasons for that. From an agricultural and ecological standpoint, some of them might be pests or spread unwanted diseases. At other times, they might be endangered and protected. In addition, not having the import ban on certain species in place, seems to encourage importing species from areas where these are plentiful, thus causing a rapid decrease of them wherever they are imported from.

Luckily, rhinoceros beetles do not tend to fall into the category of banned animals (at least, most of them do not). However, the first thing you need to consider if you are ordering from a different country is whether or not it's legal to import the species you intend on keeping. Within some countries, such as the U.S., this might apply even to transferring beetles across borders to a different state. Having said that, you might be able to keep a local species of the same kind, provided that it's not protected by law in some respect.

Another thing to keep in mind is that, even if it is legal to import a specific species, it is, more often than not, illegal to release it into the local habitat.

When it comes to keeping the local species, the general rule of thumb is that you can keep it if it is not protected by the law (for example, it's not endangered) or banned by the law (such as pests or dangerous animals).

As an example, in the United States, rhinoceros beetles are generally not protected by the Endangered Species Act signed in December of 1973. This is good news as animals that are protected under this act are either illegal to keep or they require a special permit or license to keep in the United States.

According to the U.S. Fish and Wildlife Service, the purpose of the Endangered Species Act is to "protect and recover imperiled species and the ecosystems upon which they depend". If you check the list of animals protected under the act, you shouldn't find any rhinoceros beetles on the list. This doesn't necessarily mean that they are legal to keep, however. It depends on the specific species you are thinking of buying and on where exactly you live within the United States.

Most countries have their own version of "Endangered Species Act" and the beetle you're planning on keeping should not be on it. For example, the European Union follows the so-called Bern Convention. This convention was issued by the Council of Europe and its focus is the conservation of wildlife and natural habitats in Europe.

Many countries worldwide have also signed the Convention on International Trade in Endangered Species of Wild Fauna and Flora (CITES) . While most rhinoceros beetles are neither threatened nor endangered, there are some beetles that are. If you want to find out whether the beetle species you plan to keep is endangered or threatened, the International Union for Conservation of Nature (IUCN) is where you should find out. The IUCN is the world's authority on the question of conservation. So, simply type the taxonomical name of your pet beetle into the IUCN Red List website (www.iucnredlist.org) and hopefully, you won't find it there.

A good example that deserves caution from a legal standpoint (although not a rhinoceros beetle) is *Lucanus cervus* – the stag beetle native to Europe. It can be found on the IUCN Red List of Threatened Species which lists it as near threatened. However, there are countries where stag beetle is not endangered – at least, not all species. This is, for instance, the case of Australia. Although import of foreign insects is not allowed, the country has endemic stag and rhino beetles that it allows to both breed and export.

As stated earlier, rhinoceros beetles are not endangered, but they are sometimes considered an agricultural pest. Again, to use the U.S. as an example, the United States Department of Agriculture (USDA) has a program in place called the Plant Protection and Quarantine (PPQ) program that requires a permit to import or transport any species that is considered a threat to agricultural or natural resources in the United States. If you are thinking about purchasing a beetle from outside the U.S. or are having one shipped to you, you'll need to know the following information in order to apply for a PPQ 526 permit from the USDA Animal and Plant Health Inspection Service (AHPIS):

- Is the organism indigenous to the U.S.?

- Is the organism indigenous to the area where you plan to keep it?
- What is the size and mobility of the organism?
- What is the life stage of the organism being moved?
- How many organisms are being shipped?
- Do you plan to maintain a colony or destroy them when they arrive?

If you are shipping live beetles, larvae or eggs, the package must be inspected by USDA officials upon entry to the country and they cannot contain any plant material, soil, or insect pests that aren't authorized by the permit. You do not need a permit for dead insects! For more information about USDA permits to import insects, contact Animal and Plant Health Inspection Service (APHIS) via email at this address: pest.permits@aphis.usda.gov.

When purchasing rhinoceros beetles or larvae inside the United States, you may not have to worry about getting a permit unless you are moving them across state lines. You should still make sure, however, that the species you're buying isn't protected. You should also be aware that some species of rhinoceros beetle are native to the United States, so they might require a permit to keep. This may be true for the Hercules beetle because it is native to the Eastern United States. If in doubt, it's best to contact APHIS or your state office.

The United States is a country with fairly strict rules when it comes to importing beetles. But I decided to offer it as an example for the reader to consider the different factors that may come into play when keeping beetles in your own country.

To summarize, here are the basic generic guidelines to keeping beetles:

1) You can keep local species if they are not protected by law (endangered) or banned by law (pests).

2) You can keep foreign species if the specific species is not illegal to keep in your country AND if its import isn't illegal.

3) Even if a species is allowed to be kept/bred on the national level, local authorities (such as provinces or states within a certain country) might still forbid it by law.

4) Exceptions are sometimes allowed by law. It is usually these exceptions that require the issue of a special permit or license.

Chapter 8: Setting Up Your Beetle Habitat

Adult rhinoceros beetles require different care than developing larvae. You will learn all the details for how to raise beetle larvae later in this book but, for now, let's focus on caring for your adult beetles. Rhinoceros beetles are very easy to care for – this is part of what makes them popular – but there are some dos and don'ts you should be aware of.

In this chapter, you will understand the basics about what kind of habitat is best for rhinoceros beetles in captivity. You will find out how to set up your beetle's habitat and how to keep it clean and properly maintained.

1. Basic Supplies and Equipment

When it comes to gathering supplies and equipment to create your beetle habitat, you don't have to worry about it being a long list – you only need a few things. First and foremost, you'll need some sort of tank or container to serve as your beetle housing. At a minimum, you want the tank to be at least five times as long as your beetle, both in height and width. As a general rule, however, bigger is better. If you want to make things easy, just buy a 10-gallon (40l) tank.

In addition to choosing what to use as your beetle habitat, you also have to think about decorating it. You'll need to line the bottom of the tank with at least 2 inches (5cm) of moist substrate that your beetle can dig through. For other decorations, you really only need a handful of leaves, as well as some twigs or branches your beetle can climb on. If you want to go the extra mile, you can plant live plants in the tank but know that your beetle will probably eat them.

In terms of equipment for your beetle habitat, all you need is something to keep the tank warm and humid. In most cases, a simple incandescent light fixture will work just fine. You can purchase a lamp clip or buy the kind of fixture that sits on top of the tank. Just make sure that you place it so your beetle won't be able to get close enough to be burned by the lamp as it will emit some heat.

Another option for heating your beetle tank is to install an under-tank heater. Remember to add enough substrate as to keep your beetle from coming into close contact with the heat source. You'll also want a tank thermometer to keep an eye on the tank temperature and a plastic spray bottle you can use to mist the tank with fresh water to keep the humidity up. Anything else you want to add to your beetle tank is up to you!

2. How to Set Up Your Beetle Habitat

Once you have gathered the supplies and equipment mentioned in the previous section, your next step is to put it all together. First, make sure that your beetle tank is thoroughly cleaned and dried. If you've used the tank for something else, give it a good cleaning and disinfect it with a mild bleach solution. Whatever cleaning products you use, thoroughly rinse the tank so that none of the residue remains.

After you've cleaned the tank, fill it with at least 2 inches (5cm) of moist substrate. Rich potting soil is usually a good option because it holds moisture well and it is easy for your rhino beetle to burrow into. You could also mix some sphagnum moss in with the soil to help with humidity. Once you've filled the tank with substrate, add a handful of dry leaves or bark chips and decorate with twigs and branches.

When it comes to installing your equipment, your tank lighting is pretty much the only thing you need to worry about. Your best bet is to place the light over one side of the tank and arrange the twigs below it so your beetle can get closer to the light to warm itself. The other side of the tank can be left cool. This is the only way your beetle will be able to regulate his body temperature, so make sure your tank has a warm and a cool side.

In addition to knowing what to include in your beetle habitat, you should also be mindful of the things you should NOT include. For example, you don't want a bowl of water in the tank. It might seem like adding a bowl of water will help with humidity, but you run the risk of your beetle accidentally drowning itself in it.

The next section will show you how to clean and maintain your beetle habitat.

3. Cleaning and Maintenance

Keeping your rhinoceros beetle enclosure clean is fairly easy. Not only do rhinoceros beetles have very low care requirements, but they don't tend to eat very much as adults. This being the case, you won't have to worry about changing your substrate multiple times a week or performing a total cleaning of the cage. Spot-cleaning to remove dung should be all you really need to do.

Though you don't have to worry too much about keeping your beetle cage clean, you should be mindful to keep the temperature and humidity within the proper range. The best temperature for a rhinoceros beetle tank is 68°F to 78°F (20°C to 26°C). As it has already been mentioned, you can maintain this temperature simply by installing an incandescent light fixture. In terms of humidity, aim for about 70%. Keep the substrate moist to the touch but not wet. Giving it a quick spritz once or twice a day should be adequate to maintain this humidity as long as the tank stays warm enough.

Another point to keep in mind is that you'll have to adjust the size and arrangement of your beetle habitat if you plan to keep more than one rhinoceros beetle at a time. Before you even think about keeping more than one rhinoceros beetle, however, you need to make sure that you only have one male. Multiple females can be safely housed together but male beetles will be very territorial and might fight to the death!

In addition to keeping your beetle tank warm and humid, you should be on the lookout for insect pests like mites, fruit flies, and gnats. You'll learn more about common pests for rhinoceros beetles in a later chapter on this very topic.

Chapter 9: Feeding Rhinoceros Beetles

Now that you know the basics about housing your rhinoceros beetle, you may be wondering what you need to feed it. Unlike traditional pets, beetles don't need a commercial diet and you can buy the foods your beetle needs at the grocery store. In this chapter, you'll learn the basics about what rhinoceros beetles eat in the wild and what you can feed them in captivity. You'll also learn the difference between feeding rhinoceros beetle larvae and feeding them as adults.

1. What Do Rhinoceros Beetles Eat?

In order to keep your rhinoceros beetle healthy, you need to feed it a diet that mimics what it would eat in the wild. Wild rhinoceros beetles feed primarily on tree sap, though they will also eat fruit from time to time. In captivity, however, it is much easier to feed your beetle fresh fruit. You can test out different fruits, if you like, to see what your beetle prefers but most will eat fresh apple or banana.

If you'd like to give your beetle a little more diet variety, you can also create a mixture of 3 parts mashed banana, 1 part maple syrup, and 1 part plain yogurt. This is the mixture typically fed to stag beetles but some rhinoceros beetles will eat it, too. Just offer a small amount as a supplement to your beetle's fruit. Many pet shops (even online) offer pre-packaged portions of beetle jelly. This is another way to introduce more variety into your beetle's diet.

Rhinoceros beetle adults follow a much different diet than beetle larvae. As rhinoceros beetle larvae develop, they will subsist on a diet of rotting wood. They won't be interested in tree sap or fruit. They may also eat rotting leaf litter, so plan to provide a combination of both.

2. Tips for Feeding Your Rhinoceros Beetle

One thing to remember is that larvae tend to eat a lot more than adult beetles, so you'll have to adjust your feeding strategy based on the life stage of your rhino beetle. You'll also need to remember that adult beetles eat different food than larvae.

If you're raising your beetles from larvae, your best bet is to raise them in a grow tank filled with a mixture of substrate and food. For rhinoceros beetle larvae, food consists of rotting wood and rotting leaf litter. You can purchase these supplies online and mix them at a ratio of 90% rotting wood and 10% leaf litter. Once you have that mixture, mix equal parts with rich potting soil or a coconut fiber substrate and fill your grow tank with about 6 inches (15cm) of the mixture.

Feeding your adult rhinoceros beetles is extremely easy. All you need is to put a small piece of fruit or two in the tank once a day. Also, don't forget about the pre-packaged beetle jelly that was mentioned earlier which can be easily obtained online. Although it might be a little time consuming to keep reordering the beetle jelly, the good thing about these jelly pots is that they don't attract pests.

It's practical to place the food or jelly pots for your beetle on a log or a rock in the tank, rather than the substrate itself. That way, if the food does end up attracting pests such as fruit flies, you won't have to change the whole substrate. Wooden jelly holders are available in many online stores (see the resources section at the end of this book).

When it comes to feeding your adult rhinoceros beetle, you need to be aware that it doesn't need to eat a lot each day. If you give it too much food, it's only going to attract fruit flies or other cage pests. After you've had your beetle for a week or so, you'll get a feel for how much it eats and you can adjust how much food you offer in accordance with that. This way you can avoid having too much uneaten food sitting around in the tank, rotting and attracting pests.

One more point to repeat here when it comes to feeding rhinoceros beetles is that you don't want to offer any liquid. Rhinoceros beetles do not drink water. As mentioned before, a bowl of water in the tank is only going to pose a danger – your beetle could fall in and drown. If you're worried about keeping up the humidity in your tank, the better option is to add some sphagnum moss to the tank and spritz it with fresh water once or twice a day.

Chapter 10: Health and Wellness

As an animal owner, it is your job to provide for your beetle's basic needs and to ensure that it remains in good health. This is easy enough if you own a cat or a dog – you can just take them to the vet should they gets sick. But what happens if your rhinoceros beetle falls ill? And can beetles even get sick in the first place?

In this chapter, you will get an overview of the basics about rhinoceros beetle health and wellness. We'll talk about some simple tips to keep your beetle healthy, including tips for getting rid of cage pests.

1. Does the Rhinoceros Beetle Get Sick?

As you probably know, the human body has a strong immune system that exists to help fight off harmful pathogens that could make you sick. When you are exposed to a disease or illness, your body launches an immune response to eradicate the threat. In cases where your immune system is not strong enough, or if it has never encountered a certain pathogen before, you might end up getting sick anyway.

Though there is still a lot to learn about how insects do or don't get sick, scientists have been able to determine that insects actually have very effective immune systems. For example, when an insect sustains a physical injury, the insect's immune system immediately dispatches blood cells to the site of injury to attack any invading bacteria. At the same time, an anatomical structure called the fat body begins producing high levels of antibacterial proteins for an extra layer of protection.

So, what is the answer to the question, "Does the rhinoceros beetle get sick"? In theory, insects are just as capable of sustaining injury or developing disease as humans and other mammals are. Bacteria, viruses, and other pathogens are just as potentially harmful to insects as to humans. Think about some of the deadliest diseases in human history – diseases like malaria and Zika virus. These diseases are carried by insects and transferred to humans. The disease may or may not affect the insect itself, but this example shows that insects can, in fact, be affected by some of the same harmful pathogens known to affect humans.

The good news is that rhinoceros beetles, like other insects, have strong immune systems. In fact, the insect immune system works in a similar way as the human immune system. This also means that insects can, theoretically, be treated for disease. When it comes to the relationship between insects and disease, however, most research is focused on getting rid of the insects themselves because they are the source of disease or damage. This is particularly true in the field of agriculture. There is very little research devoted to diseases that affect insects themselves – insects like the rhinoceros beetle.

2. Pathogens that Affect Rhinoceros Beetles

Beetles can be affected by harmful pathogens – primarily bacteria. Keep in mind, though, that insects like the rhinoceros beetle are most likely to encounter these pathogens in the wild. Many of them are used commercially in the agriculture industry to control insect pests. It is, nonetheless, still a good idea to familiarize yourself with these pathogens, so you can keep your beetle healthy.

In this section, you'll get an overview of some of the pathogens that are most harmful to insects like the rhinoceros beetle.

A. *Bacillus thuringiensis*

A naturally-occurring bacteria, *Bacillus thuringiensis* are one of the most commonly used bacteria for natural insect control. Back in the last century, scientists developed an insecticide based on *Bacillus thuringiensis* which produces spores and toxic proteins. When insects like the rhinoceros beetle ingest the bacteria, the toxic protein is released in the insect's gut where it prevents the stomach from producing digestive juices. As a result, the insect dies from poisoning. Though deadly to insects, *Bacillus thuringiensis* is completely harmless to fish, birds, and other mammals.

B. *Bacillus popilliae*

In the 1900s, the Japanese beetle (*Popillia japonica*) was introduced in the United States and spread quickly, doing a great deal of damage. By the 1930s, the problem had become so severe that scientists were asked to develop a control measure. The result of their research was the discovery of the *Bacillus popilliae* bacteria which caused a disease called milky spore.

The *Bacillus popilliae* bacteria can be spread in the form of spores to control insect pests like the Japanese beetle. When the larvae of the beetle ingest the bacterial spores, they germinate and begin to reproduce inside the larvae's body, eventually killing it. When the dead larvae decompose, the spores are spread in the soil to kill eggs and other larvae, preventing them from developing into adults. Because these bacteria are so effective against Japanese beetles, it is something to watch out for when it comes to protecting the health of your rhinoceros beetle.

C. *Rhabdionvirus oryctes*

Though many commercial bacteria applications are designed for general pest control, there is a type of insect virus that has been studied specifically for its effects against a species of rhinoceros beetle – the coconut rhinoceros beetle (*Oryctes rhinoceros*). This beetle is native to Southeast Asia and it is also known as the Asiatic rhinoceros beetle or the coconut rhinoceros beetle described earlier in this book.

In the 1960s, the coconut rhinoceros beetle became a nuisance pest in the South Pacific – it fed on coconut palm trees and devastated the population. In 1967, *Rhabdionvirus oryctes* was discovered in larvae of the beetle which led to the development of a commercial version of the virus. It helped to control the ever-growing coconut rhinoceros beetle population.

D. *Metarhizium anisopliae*

One of the most commonly used fungal strains for insect pest control is *Metarhizium anisoplieae.* It is, plain and simple, a fungus that parasitizes insects. It is widely considered one of the best methods of microbial pest control for insects.

This fungus works by adhering to the surface of the insect host. After adhering to the insect, the fungus penetrates the exoskeleton and spreads its spores into the body where they grow and cause damage to the internal organs. Eventually, the insect host dies and the fungus spreads to another host.

3. Tips for Keeping Your Beetle Healthy

The best way to keep your rhinoceros beetle healthy is to provide for its basic needs. Ensuring that it has a large enough habitat to be comfortable will help reduce stress and making sure its diet is adequate will keep him healthy. You'll also need to clean the habitat and maintain the right degree of moisture and humidity. If you can do these things, your beetle should enjoy a happy and healthy life.

Even if you are careful to properly maintain your rhino beetle tank, you could still end up with problems. One of the most common problems affecting pet beetles, aside from dietary and habitat issues, is cage pests. Cage pests come in various forms including mites, gnats, and flies. Depending on what life stage your beetle is in, these pests could be nothing more than a minor nuisance or they could be a threat to your beetle's life.

Let's now look at the different cage pests and how to deal with them.

A. Mites

These insect pests look very much like tiny spiders. Mites are, in fact, arachnids (just like spiders) but they are more closely related to ticks. These insect pests are everywhere – they could even be on your body right now – but they don't typically pose a problem unless they begin to rapidly multiply and take over the tank. In your beetle tank, you are most likely to find mites chowing down on the uneaten food your beetle left behind. But you might also find them in your live plants, if you are using any. Some mites have also been known to feed on rhino beetle eggs, but they don't typically kill the egg by doing so.

Getting rid of mites in your rhino beetle tank can be tricky because they are so small. If you find the mites on your rhino beetle's body, use a small brush to sweep them off. It may also help to leave some food in a corner of the tank so the mites will be attracted to the food and leave your beetle alone. You should also change the substrate once a day for a few days in a row until the mites are gone. Some say that lowering the humidity in the tank will kill the mites, but it will also harm your beetle, so this method is best avoided.

B. Fungus Gnats

Though they look very similar to fruit flies, fungus gnats tend to feed on decomposing organic matter. They also feed on fungi. These tiny insects have an elongated body that tapers to a point at the end of the abdomen and they have large, translucent wings. Fungus gnats can sometimes be found on live plants, though they tend to gather over mold deposits and decaying matter. They are also likely to appear if your beetle tank becomes too humid.

Adult fungus gnats only live for about a week, but they can lay up to 300 eggs during that time. The larvae hatch within a few days and begin feeding on plant roots before they burrow into the substrate to pupate. Because these insects reproduce so quickly, they can be difficult to control. They also thrive in humid environments which is necessary for your rhinoceros beetle. You can try using sticky traps or simply change the substrate daily for as long as it takes to get rid of all the eggs and larvae.

C. Fruit Flies

Whether you've kept rhino beetles before or not, you are probably familiar with fruit flies. These tiny little flies have orange bodies and red eyes and they are attracted to decaying fruit. Unlike other flies, fruit flies will not feed on any decomposing organic matter or non-fruit foods. They only eat rotting fruit. In many cases, removing the fruit from the cage will cause the flies to seek food elsewhere, but they'll probably come back the next time you feed your beetle.

The best option to get rid of these flies is to set a trap or two near your beetle tank. Fill a small container with apple cider vinegar and add a few drops of liquid dish soap. You can also add a few pieces of fruit to make the trap more appealing. Then, put the trap near your beetle cage. The fruit flies will be attracted to the vinegar but once they try to land on the surface the soap will cause them to fall through and drown.

D. Phorid Flies

Similar to fruit flies in appearance, phorid flies have yellow-orange bodies with a banded pattern and thicker bodies. These flies are drawn to decomposing organic matter, so they may find their way into your beetle's tank if you fail to clean up when it leaves some of its food behind. Phorid flies can smell death from great distances – even from outside your house – and they will stop at nothing to get to the source. The only way to get rid of these flies is to get rid of their food source.

E. Nematodes

If you are into gardening, you may already be familiar with nematodes. Nematodes are microscopic worms that can be found in soil all over the world, even in your backyard. Though these animals are tiny, they can do a lot of damage to beetles, especially eggs and larvae. In fact, nematodes can be used as a natural remedy for controlling insect pests in the garden at home.

When it comes to nematodes and insect pets, they are most commonly seen affecting tarantulas but they have been known to cause problems for breeding beetles as well. It is very important that you never use soil from your yard in your beetle tank because you could accidentally introduce harmful nematodes. Once you have nematodes in your substrate, they can be very difficult to eradicate. You will probably need to clean the whole tank.

F. Elaterid Larvae

Insects belonging to the family *Elateridae* are also known as click beetles. These small beetles get their name from a unique behavior they exhibit – when they find themselves upside down they are able to spring into the air and land on their feet. As they do, they make a clicking noise that is surprisingly loud. These beetles are not harmful to rhinoceros beetles but their larvae can be. They have been known to damage beetle eggs and pupae.

In addition to keeping an eye out for these cage pests, you'll want to make sure your beetle tank remains free from fungus and mold. Because your beetle tank is going to be fairly moist and humid, there may be a little bit of fungus or mold present in the form of spores. These are so small that you may not even notice them. It isn't until the fungus spreads that you really see it but by that point it could already be affecting your beetle's health.

Mold often starts with a single spot, or maybe a few spots. As it spreads, it could develop into larger, fuzzy growths or it could take on a stringy, hair-like appearance. A few spots may seem like nothing to worry about but, in the right conditions, mold and fungus can spread very quickly. The mold and fungi may not harm your beetle but it is a sign that the conditions in your tank are not ideal. Remove the affected substrate or tank decorations and replace them with new, clean ones.

Though mold and fungi are more of a nuisance than an actual threat to your beetle's life, bacterial and viral infections can be dangerous. Unfortunately, there is little information out there about how bacteria affect beetles and other large insects because they don't show obvious symptoms of illness in the same way that larger animals do. In cases where very young beetles die mysteriously, bacterial infections often take the blame.

To help protect your beetle from mold, fungi, bacteria, and viruses, you need to be careful about where you source your food and tank decorations. It is unwise to collect dirt from the outdoors to use in your beetle tank because you don't know what kind of insect pests or other harmful substances it might contain. For food, avoid produce that has been treated with chemical pesticides or fertilizers and clean it thoroughly before using it. The best rule of thumb to follow is that, if you aren't completely sure it's safe for your beetle, you shouldn't use it.

Chapter 11: Breeding Rhinoceros Beetles

You've already learned the basics about the rhinoceros beetle life cycle. You understand, at least to some degree, how breeding beetles works. Breeding rhinoceros beetles is particularly interesting because they exhibit some unique behaviors as they go through the different stages of development. Breeding them is, for many beetle-lovers, the most exciting part of keeping them.

Breeding rhinoceros beetles is not particularly difficult, but it does take some preparation. In this chapter, you'll learn everything you need to know to successfully breed these beautiful beetles.

1. Rhinoceros Beetle Breeding Basics

Just a few decades ago, many of the rhinoceros beetles in the pet industry were captured in the wild. When the popularity of large pet beetles took off, they actually became quite scarce in the wild because they were so heavily collected. In the 1980s, commercial breeding of rhinoceros beetles became possible as people began to study their life cycle and breeding habits. Today, it is easy to find rhinoceros beetles for sale, along with relatively plenty of information out there to help with successful breeding.

Before you get started breeding your beetles, you should learn the basics of how to do it. Males typically take longer than females to pass from the larval stage into the pupal stage and some species take longer than others to pass from the pupal stage into adulthood.

To give you a quick idea of what the breeding timeline for rhinoceros beetles is like, here is a summary:

- Egg Incubation Stage = 3 to 4 weeks
- Larval Stage (male) = 12 to 18 months
  - L1: 1 month, L2: 2 months, L3: 9-15 months
- Larval Stage (female) = 12 months
  - L1: 1 month, L2: 2 months, L3: 9 months
- Pupal Stage = 2 to 3 months

With this basic understanding of the breeding cycle for rhinoceros beetles, let's look at the specifics. First and foremost, you'll have to obtain a male and female beetle of the same species. For the most part, the sexes are fairly easy to tell apart. Male rhino beetles are larger than females and they have enlarged jaws designed for battle. If the female has them, they are much smaller than the male's. Male beetles may also have bushy antennae to distinguish them.

Once you've obtained a male and female beetle, the next step is to create a breeding tank. In most cases, rhino beetles breed readily when placed in the correct environment. Keep reading to learn more about how to set up a breeding tank for rhinoceros beetles and how to raise and breed them from larvae.

2. Setting Up a Breeding Tank

Provided they are healthy, male and female rhinoceros beetles should breed readily when they are placed together. This being the case, you don't need a special tank for breeding. You can simply put the two beetles together in a container and they should mate fairly quickly. The mating process can last for up to an hour and it usually only takes one mating for the female to become gravid. Once this happens, separate her into an egg laying chamber.

An egg laying chamber for gravid female rhinoceros beetles can be made from any large plastic or glass container. If you plan to rear the larvae yourself, you'll probably want to just set up a larvae rearing tank to use as the egg laying chamber so you can simply remove the female after she lays her eggs instead of transferring the eggs to another container. Once she lays her eggs, you can keep the female in the rearing tank for three to four weeks, but you should remove her before the eggs hatch.

The two primary things you need for a rhinoceros beetle larvae rearing tank, is the tank itself and some substrate. The tank doesn't need to be huge, but it should be large enough for the female to find space to deposit up to 50 eggs. A glass fish tank is usually a good option, as long as it has a lid so the beetles can't escape. Look for something in the range of 10 to 15 gallons (40 to 60l). You can also use an empty kitty litter tub or a plastic storage tub.

Once you have your tank, you'll need to fill it with substrate and then add your larvae. There are several different kinds of substrate you can use but rich gardening soil is the best option. Keep in mind that you'll also have to provide the larvae with food, so mix the garden soil with rotten wood at a ratio of 2-to-1. The soil itself should be free from fertilizers and pesticides. It should also contain a little bit of sand.

When it comes to the rotten wood for your larvae rearing tank, you need to be careful. Avoid wood from pines and other conifers because they contain chemicals that can be toxic to your beetles. Stick with hardwood. To start the wood rotting, you'll need to do some planning so it's ready when the larvae hatch.

Don't collect rotting wood from outdoors because it is likely to contain mites, ants, or other creatures that could eat the eggs. Simply collect some dry hardwood and soak it in containers of water for at least 1 week. After soaking, freeze the wood for a week or two and then break it into small pieces and mix it with your soil. Another option is to buy the substrate online. It usually sells as "larva substrate" and is often boosted with nutrients suitable for the larvae.

Once you have your soil and wood mixture, fill the tank with 6 inches (15cm) of it at the very least and pack it in well. It is sometimes recommended to double the amount up to 12-16 inches (30-40cm). Without enough substrate, the female may lay fewer eggs or she may lay no eggs at all. The substrate needs to be packed in enough that the larvae can burrow into it to complete the pupal stage but not packed so tight that it isn't aerated. When your tank is ready, add the female beetle to the tank and let her deposit her eggs. Humidity is key when it comes to the eggs. Don't be surprised if you see them increase their size by more than double in a matter of a couple of days. This is due to the eggs absorbing the water present in their environment.

As you have already learned, the larval stage in the rhinoceros beetle life cycle can last for over a year. Throughout that time, you'll want to change the substrate from time to time and make sure to keep it moist. Check the substrate daily to ensure that it is moist to the touch because if it dries out, your larvae will die. How often you change the substrate is up to you, but you can tell that it needs to be done when you start to see dung accumulating in the substrate. Larger tanks will need to have their substrate refreshed less often than smaller tanks. But a good rule of thumb is to change the substrate once a month. If you use a filter, you will be able to discard the excrements while keeping substrate that is still usable. But even then, change the substrate completely every three months or so.

3. Rearing Beetle Larvae

As you wait for your larvae to develop, you should keep the substrate moist and maintain humidity inside the tank. The ideal temperature range for rearing rhinoceros beetle larvae is 68°F to 78°F (20°C to 26°C). If you keep the rearing tank indoors, you shouldn't have trouble maintaining this temperature but, if you do, you can try placing a lamp over the tank to keep it warm.

Over the next 12 to 18 months, your larvae will develop and go through the three substages of the larval development. During this time, make sure your larvae have plenty of food because they are going to eat a lot! In addition to mixing rotten wood with the substrate you can provide rotten apples or rotten leaves. Some people use dog food as well, but with that you run the risk of attracting mites or other pests.

As your larvae approach the end of their development, they'll start to wander. At this point, you'll need to separate them into individual pupal chambers where they can complete their development. Each grub should be placed in its own container with just enough soil to fill it halfway. Empty plastic ice cream containers are perfect for that. That way, you will avoid the occasional cannibalism and competition for food. Be extra careful when transferring your larvae into individual containers as they are extremely vulnerable at this stage of development.

After your larvae enter the pupal stage, it will take them two to three months to develop and emerge as adult beetles. It is advisable to add in some sand into the substrate in order to help create a more solid layer. Its function is to protect the larva that is now getting ready to emerge as an adult beetle. Once again remember to be extra careful when manipulating with the larvae at this stage, as they might not be able to repair the damage caused by rough manipulation and they may die. There are those of us – beetle enthusiasts – who stay away from touching the larvae with bare hands completely. This is because the bacteria residing on human skin can potentially damage the larvae just as much as rough manipulation. There is no more need to change the substrate or to provide extra food at this point.

Keep in mind that when they first emerge, the beetles will not have a fully hardened exoskeleton. Beetles in this stage are called "teneral" adults and they may not actually leave the soil. You'll need to turn the soil every few days to see if the beetle has emerged.

It is recommended to keep only one male rhino beetle in the tank, along with 2 or 3 females. Rhino beetles are fairly territorial and fight for the females if you place more than one male in your tank.

Some people go as far as rearing males and females separately all the time and putting them together only once they would like them to mate.

Chapter 12: Stag Beetles

Stag beetle is not a species of the rhinoceros beetle subfamily, but it does belong to the same superfamily of beetles called Scarabaeoidea. The name stag beetle applies to about 1,200 different species of beetles in the family Lucanidae and they are divided into four subfamilies.

For the most part, these beetles reach a length of about 2 inches (5cm), but some species achieve lengths of 4.7 inches (12cm) or more. They are not quite as large or thick-bodied as rhinoceros beetles, but they do have a set of large pincers similar to the rhino beetle's horn.

It is due to their impressive (and maybe scary) appearance that the stag beetle was believed, in some cultures, to have the power to summon thunder and lightning. In fact, there are many legends and stories, especially in the European folklore, that surround this beetle. As an example, he was attributed the ability to carry hot coals to houses, causing domestic fire. This is why they were not welcome in people's homes. In other parts of Europe, though, they were considered good luck charms or protection charms against evil. One way or another, it seems like the stag beetle didn't leave people in Europe indifferent.

Like some species of rhinoceros beetle, stag beetles are sexually dimorphic. Male stag beetles have enlarged mandibles that look like pincers but they are actually too weak to do much damage (although with some species caution might be in order). Though the female has much smaller mandibles, she is capable of a painful bite. Male stag beetles use their mandibles primarily for fighting other males.

As many other beetles, the stag beetle has a major positive influence on the environment, cleaning our gardens and forests of rotting matter such as leaves, fruit or wood.

When it comes to keeping stag beetles as pets or hobby (provided you made sure they are legal to keep in your country), they require a little more care than rhinoceros beetles. However, they do live longer than rhino beetles.

Start with a tank or tub large enough to keep your beetle comfortable and then fill it with about 2 inches (5cm) of rich soil or coconut fiber substrate. If you are breeding stag beetles, you'll need to make the bedding a few inches deeper. On top of the bedding, add some decorations like dry leaves, branches, and logs.

The most important aspect of caring for stag beetles is maintaining the proper temperature and humidity because these beetles dehydrate very easily. The ideal temperature range is 68°F to 77°F (20°C to 25°C) and you should keep your beetle tank out of direct sunlight.

Feeding a stag beetle is very similar to feeding rhinoceros beetles. Just offer small amounts of fresh fruits like bananas and apples. Do not offer high-moisture fruits like watermelon. You can also make a mix of 3 parts mashed banana, 1 part maple syrup, and 1 part plain yogurt to offer your beetle in small amounts or buy some beetle jelly. When it comes to stag beetle diet, there are several question marks even amongst experts. For example, they are not quite sure about what exactly these beetles eat after they transform into adults and if they eat at all in the wild once they have reached adulthood.

Something else you should remember about stag beetles is that they live much longer than rhinoceros beetles. The development from egg to adult may still take several years, but these beetles tend to live 3 to 5 years on average. Some have even lived 8 years in captivity.

Also, keep in mind that these beetles hibernate during the winter. Your beetle will burrow into the soil to hibernate so be sure to keep it moist and don't let the temperature drop too low.

If you plan to breed your stag beetles, you'll need to acquire a male and a female and prepare your tank with extra-deep substrate. To breed stag beetles, make sure you wait until they naturally finish hibernating. In the wild, the adults usually emerge from late May to the beginning of August. At this point, you can put your male and female beetles together and wait for them to mate. After being gravid for a few weeks, the female will deposit her eggs on a piece of decaying wood buried in the substrate.

Stag beetle larvae are C-shaped with a soft, almost transparent cream-colored body with six orange legs and an orange head. They also have a pair of brown, very sharp pincers. The larval stage for stag beetles is even longer than the rhinoceros beetle's –

about 4 to 6 years – and it still involves several substages. Once the larvae become pupae, they develop in the soil over a period of about three months at which point they emerge to find a mate.

1. Popular Stag Beetle Species

As you already know, there are about 1,200 different species of stag beetle. Not all of them, however, are popular as pets. Stag beetles are divided into four subfamilies:

- *Aesalinae*
- *Lampriminae*
- *Lucaninae*
- *Syndesinae*

One of the most commonly known species is *Lucanus cervus*. This beetle is native throughout Europe. It is, however, either endangered or absent from its European habitat which is why it's illegal to keep it as a pet in most European countries.

In its natural habitat, these beetles are typically found in certain trees belonging to beech, willow and walnut families.

Apart from *Lucanus cervus* which is primarily known throughout Europe, there are also a few species native to the United States and Canada.

The giant stag beetle (*Lucanus elaphus*) is also known as the elk stag beetle. This species is the largest and the most recognizable species of stag beetle in the United States, easy to identify by the giant set of pincers possessed by males. These beetles use their massive mandibles to fight with other males, specifically as a tool to pry each other off of a log, dropping the other to the ground. The mandibles are not actually used for biting or pinching.

Giant stag beetles have shiny dark brown bodies and their heads and mandibles are a little bit lighter in color. Males generally grow between 1.1 and 2.3 inches (28 to 60mm) long, including the mandibles. This species is found throughout Virginia, North Carolina, South Carolina, and Oklahoma. They tend to be found in wooded areas where larvae feed on the dead or decaying wood of stumps and logs. They aren't commonly seen in the wild, even though they are the largest beetle in North America .   .

Another stag beetles found in the United States that is easy to identify by its large mandibles is the reddish-brown stag beetle (*Lucanus capreolus*). The reddish-brown stag beetle is the second largest stag beetle in terms of size. These beetles are sometimes called pinching bugs because their mandibles are curved inward and they both come to a sharp point. Though female reddish-brown stag beetles look almost identical to female elephant stag beetles, the males are easy to distinguish because their mandibles have distinctly different shapes and lengths.

Reddish-brown stag beetles usually grow between 0.9 to 1.6 inches (22 to 40mm) in length and they are, as the name suggests, reddish-brown in color. Larvae feed on decaying wood and take several years to fully develop from larvae into adults. As adults, they eat very little and only live for a year or two. In comparison, giant stag beetles grow up to 2.3 inches (60mm) and they are also reddish brown in color. Male beetles have much longer mandibles and each one has three prongs. The mandibles typically grow more than half as long as the beetle's body.

Of course, there are stag beetles elsewhere in the world, too. In Australia alone, there are almost 90 different species of stag beetle. In fact, this chapter wouldn't be complete without, at least, mentioning the magnificent rainbow stag beetle (*Phalacrognathus muelleri*) found mostly in Australia. Apart from its impressive appearance, it is also the largest member of the Lucanidae family on the Australian continent. The rainbow stag beetle may well end up being one of the most beautiful beetles you'll ever see.

The stag beetle is considered to be globally threatened which is why it can be found on the red list of many countries and there are several reasons for this. First of all, it's already extinct in some countries. Then, there is climate change, as well as people killing them off simply because they look scary. However, the biggest threat is the loss of its natural habitat, especially the woodlands.

2. Summary of Stag Beetle Facts

Common Name: stag beetle

Scientific Name: Lucanidae

Habitat: Europe, North and South America, Africa, Asia, Australia

Size: average 2 inches (5cm), up to 4.7 inches (12cm)

Lifespan: average 3 to 5 years, up to 8 years

Housing: tank or terrarium at least 5x body length

Temperature: 68°F to 77°F (20°C to 25°C)

Humidity: 70%

Chapter 13: Goliath Beetles

Though the Goliath beetle belongs to a different subfamily than the rhinoceros beetle, they are often popularly grouped together because they are both very large in size. Similar to the stag beetle, this species may or may not be allowed to keep in your country, so check the law before procuring one to keep as a pet or as a hobby.

The name Goliath beetle applies to five species in the genus *Goliathus* and they are named after the biblical giant Goliath. This name is fitting because these beetles range in size from 2 to 4.5 inches (5 to 11.5cm) in length and they can weigh as much as 3.5 ounces (100g).

Goliath beetles belong to the subfamily Cetoniinae which is in the family Scarabaeidae – the same family as rhinoceros beetles (although not the same family as the stag beetles). Primarily found in Africa's tropical forests, these beetles feed on tree sap and fruit. As is true for rhinoceros beetles, little is known about the life cycle of these beetles in the wild but they have been successfully reared in captivity time and time again.

The Goliath beetle has a massive body and, like all other beetles, a pair of elytra which act both as a secondary set of wings and protective cover for the abdomen. It is only the larger pair of wings that is used for flying, however. The Goliath beetle's legs are large, and each one ends in a pair of sharp claws that can be used for grip during climbing. The male Goliath beetle also possesses a Y-shaped horn on the head that can be used during battle. Female Goliath beetles do not have a horn and they have a more wedge-shaped head that they use for burrowing to lay their eggs.

Breeding Goliath beetles is relatively easy in captivity, though the details of their breeding in the wild are still somewhat a mystery. In most cases, a male and female beetle will breed readily as soon as they are put together. After mating, the female will be gravid for an average of four to six weeks before burrowing into the substrate and depositing her eggs at the lowest level. These beetles deposit their eggs singly in small nodules of compacted substrate. You can tell that egg laying has begun when the female starts digging vertical tunnels in the tank substrate.

After the eggs have been deposited, they usually hatch after 12 to 14 days. At this point, the larvae go through three substages. During the larval stage, the Goliath beetles will grow up to 5 inches (13cm) long and can achieve a weight of 3.5 ounces (100g) or more. The entire larval stage usually lasts for up to two years, though it may vary slightly by species and sex.

After completing the larval stage, Goliath beetles enter pupation. For a long time, the details of this stage were an enigma but now it is known that, in captivity, the larvae will start to make attempts at escaping their container when they are ready to pupate. At this point, they should be transferred to smaller containers in which they can build their pupal cell. It may take as long as 7 to 10 days for the larvae to settle down and, once it does, the pupal stage lasts for about 8 to 10 weeks.

Once the Goliath beetle larvae have finished pupating, they will remain in their pupal cell for hibernation period lasting 3 to 4 months. In the wild, this coincides with the arrival of the wet season. During this time, the young beetle's exoskeleton will thicken and darken. When the adult beetle emerges, you can expect an average lifespan of 6 to 8 months, though they can live up to a year.

1. Goliath Beetle Species

The Goliath beetle has its own separate genus, *Goliathus*, and there are five different species. These beetles are found throughout Africa, feeding on the fruit and sap of tropical forest trees. Here is the list of the five species:

- *Goliathus goliatus*
- *Goliathus albosignatus*
- *Goliathus regius*
- *Goliathus cacicus*
- *Goliathus orientalis*

The first of these species, *Goliathus goliatus*, grow up to 4.3 inches (11cm) in length in males, while females only grow to about 3.1 inches (8cm). The thoracic shield, also known as the pronotum, is black in color with longitudinal stripes and the elytra are a dark brown. The head is white in color with a black Y-shaped horn in males of the species. These beetles also possess a secondary pair of membranous wings that they use for flying. These are kept folded under the elytra when they are not in use.

The *Goliathus goliatus* beetle is widespread throughout equatorial Africa and while it primarily lives in the forest, it can also be found in the sub-equatorial savannah. The specimens that live in the savannah are typically found in shady areas. Some of the countries in which this species is found include Cameroon, the Republic of Congo, the Central African Republic, Gabon, Kenya, the Democratic Republic of Congo, Nigeria, Tanzania, and Uganda.

The next species, *Goliathus albosignatus,* is the smallest of the five Goliath beetles. These beetles range from about 1.8 to 2.8 inches (4.5 to 7cm) in males and from 1.6 to 2 inches (4 to 5cm) in females. This species exhibits a series of undulating, horizontal black bands on the elytra with a yellow or tan overall color. They tend to live in various parts of Malawi, South Africa, Zimbabwe, Tanzania, and Mozambique. They are common in some parts of this range but, overall, they are one of the less often encountered species of Goliath beetle.

The *Goliathus regius* species is also known as the royal Goliath beetle and it is very similar to the *Goliathus goliatus* in size, structure, as well as color. These beetles range from 2 to 4.3 inches (5 to 11cm) in males with females being slightly smaller. This species has a broad, flat body and the thoracic shield has a large, black longitudinal stripe down the middle. The elytra are white in color with a complex pattern of dark markings and the head exhibits a Y-shaped horn in males of the species.

The royal Goliath beetle is found in parts of western equatorial Africa such as Ghana, Guinea, Burkina Faso, Nigeria, Ivory Coast, and Sierra Leone. Though relatively little is known about the breeding habits of this species in the wild, the larvae are known to live buried in the soil and they require a very protein-rich diet in order to thrive because they grow more quickly than other beetles. In captivity, royal Goliath beetle larvae are often fed dog or cat food and they take about 4 months to fully mature. In the wild, this period coincides with the rainy season.

The next species, *Goliathus cacicus*, is found throughout Ghana, Burkina Faso, Guinea, Liberia, Nigeria, Sierra Leone, and the Ivory Coast. This beetle grows between 2 and 3.9 inches in males (5 to 10cm) and up to 2.8 inches in females (up to 7cm). These beetles are more brown in color than other Goliath beetles and they don't exhibit the same degree of horizontal banding on the thoracic shield.

The *Goliathus orientalis* species is another very large beetle, measuring 2 to 3.9 inches (5 to 10cm) in length for males and 2 to 2.6 inches (5 to 6.5cm) in females. These beetles have a broad, flat body with whitish elytra that are covered in a complex pattern of dark markings, often in the shape of rings. There is also a longitudinal black stripe on the thoracic shield, as is true for many goliath beetles.

Like the royal Goliath beetle, this species takes about 4 months to mature as larvae and they need a very protein-rich diet. The larvae can grow up to 5.1 inches (13cm) in length and can weigh up to 3.5 ounces (100g). When the larvae reach their maximum size, they create a pupal cell in which the undergo the process of metamorphosis to become adult beetles. They spend most of the dry season in this pupal cell and the adult beetle typically doesn't emerge until the rainy season starts. In captivity, they live for about a year but their lives in the wild are much shorter.

2. Summary of Goliath Beetle Facts

Common Name: Goliath beetle

Scientific Name: *Goliathus*

Habitat: Africa

Size: 2 to 4.5 inches (5 to 11.5cm) long

Weight: up to 3.5 ounces (100g)

Lifespan: 6 to 8 months average, up to 12 months as adults

Housing: tank or terrarium at least 5x body length

Temperature: 75°F to 82°F (24°C to 28°C)

Humidity: 70%

Chapter 14: Relevant Websites

Hopefully, you have a clear idea by now whether the rhinoceros beetle is the right beetle for you or not. If so, you're ready to move to the next step – buying your supplies, equipment, and beetles!

You've already received some general advice for finding these things but, in this chapter, you'll be able to access specific resources for everything you need including tanks and supplies, food, and your beetles themselves.

The websites that follow were selected because they use English as their language (since this book is written in English). Naturally, you might be able to find local online stores using the language of your country in your online search.

1. Rhinoceros Beetle Tanks and Supplies

To ensure that your rhinoceros beetle is properly cared for, you need to provide it with a suitable habitat. Here are some resources to purchase beetle tanks and other supplies:

Coleoptera XXL.

<http://www.coleoptera-xxl.de/cgi-bin/shop/frontEN/shop_main.cgi?func=rubrik&wkid=3019715060951415&rub1=Substrate>

BioQuip Products.

<https://www.bioquip.com/Search/WebCatalog.asp?category=2850&prodtype=1>

Bugs in Cyberspace.

<http://shop.bugsincyberspace.com/Complete-Pet-Bug-Habitat-Kits_c29.htm> U.S. based customers only

Insect Cage Plan.

<http://www.craftsmanspace.com/free-projects/insect-cage-plan.html>

National History and Book Service.
<https://www.nhbs.com/equipment/insect-cages>

The Spider Shop.

<http://www.thespidershop.co.uk/equipment-c-36.html>

Rhino Beetle U.K.

<https://www.rhinobeetle.co.uk/index.php/shop/categories-2>

Peregrine Live Foods.

<https://shop.peregrine-livefoods.co.uk/catalogue/category/16>

Bugzarre – Vivarium Hardware.

<http://bugzarre.co.uk/epages/950002515.sf/en_GB/?ObjectPath=
/Shops/950002515/Categories/VIV_BITS>

Small-Life.co.uk.

<http://www.small-life.co.uk/page4.html>

2. Food for Rhinoceros Beetles

Feeding your rhinoceros beetle will be different throughout his lifetime as he develops from a larva into an adult. Here are some resources to purchase food for beetles and larvae:

Flake Soil.

<http://flake-soil.com/gb/buy-flake-soil/40-white-rotten-breeding-wood-s-soft-decayed.html>

Bugs in Cyberspace.

<http://shop.bugsincyberspace.com/Dry-Food-Products_c17.htm>
U.S. based customers only

Cape Cod Roaches.

<https://capecodroaches.com/t/insect-supplies> U.S. customers
only

Beetles as Pets.

<http://beetlesaspets.blogspot.com/2013/11/jelly-for-tropical-beetles-at-home.html>

Rhino Beetle U.K. <https://www.rhinobeetle.co.uk/
index.php/shop/categories-2/adult-food/>

BeetleJelly.eu. <http://www.beetlejelly.eu/> - European Union
only

Online Reptile Shop.

< http://www.onlinereptileshop.co.uk/our-products-Jelly-Pots-and-Beetle-Jelly-196-1>

The Spider Shop.

<http://www.thespidershop.co.uk/livefood-care-diets-c-65_70.html?osCsid=63c4b09f3692c28b77ae3a8d822e7c6c>

Bugzarre – Food and Feeding.

<http://bugzarre.co.uk/epages/950002515.sf/en_GB/?ObjectPath=
/Shops/950002515/Categories/Food__Feeding>

3. Rhinoceros Beetles, Eggs, and Larvae

You won't always be able to find a rhinoceros beetle or beetle larvae at your local pet store. Here are some resources to purchase beetles, eggs, and larvae:

Coleoptera XXL.

<http://www.coleoptera-xxl.de/cgi-bin/shop/frontEN/shop_main.cgi?func=rubrik&wkid=3019715060951415&rub1=Coleoptera>

Bugs In Cyberspace.

<http://shop.bugsincyberspace.com/Beetles_c6.htm> U.S. based customers only

Rhino Beetles U.K.
<https://www.rhinobeetle.co.uk/index.php/shop/category-page>

Rakuten Global Market.

<https://global.rakuten.com/en/category/409840/>

Australian Insect Farm.

<http://www.insectfarm.com.au/pets.php>

Exotic-Pets.co.uk.

<https://www.exotic-pets.co.uk/beetles-for-sale.html>

Peregrine Life Foods.

<https://shop.peregrine-livefoods.co.uk/catalogue/product/XBEETLE3>

Index

A

B

C

D

E

F

G

H

I

J

K

L

M

N

O

P

Rhinoceros Beetles as Pets and Hobby

Q

R

S

T

U

V

W

X

Resources

"About Stag Beetles." People's Trust for Endangered Species. <https://ptes.org/campaigns/stag-beetles/stag-beetle-facts/>

"Beetle Care and Housing." Keeping Insects. <https://www.keepinginsects.com/beetle/care/>

Bouchard, Patrice. "The Evolution and Diversity of Beetles." Mother Earth News. <https://www.motherearthnews.com/nature-and-environment/wildlife/evolution-and-diversity-of-beetles-ze0z1502zdeh>

Broadley, Hannah. "Insects Get Sick Too: The Study of Insect Pathology." That's Life. <http://thatslifesci.com.s3-website-us-east-1.amazonaws.com/2016-11-10-Insects-Get-Sick-Too-Broadley/>

"Cage Pests." Bugs in Cyberspace. <http://www.bugsincyberspace.com/Cage_Pests.html>

"Care Guide." Minibeast Wildlife. <http://shop.minibeastwildlife.com.au/content/Minibeast%20Wildlife%20Care%20Guide%20-%20Xylotrupes%20ulysses.pdf>

Clark, Amy. "Top 10 Arthropod Pets." Listverse. <https://listverse.com/2012/09/26/top-10-arthropod-pets/>

"Coconut Rhinoceros Beetle." American Samoa Community College. <https://www.ctahr.hawaii.edu/adap/>

"History of Bug Keeping." Keeping Insects. <https://www.keepinginsects.com/introduction/history/>ASCC_Landgrant/Dr_Brooks/BrochureNo8.pdf>

Emlen, Douglas. "On the Origin and Diversification of Beetle Horns." PNAS. May 2007; 104(1). <http://www.pnas.org/content/104/suppl_1/8661.full>

"Endangered Species Act Overview." U.S. Fish and Wildlife Service. <https://www.fws.gov/endangered/laws-policies/>

Francisco, Aya. "How to Care for Your Beetle." Tofugu. <https://www.tofugu.com/japan/pet-beetles-in-japan/>

"Fungus Gnat." Planet Natural Research Center. <https://www.planetnatural.com/pest-problem-solver/houseplant-pests/fungus-gnat-control/>

"Giant Stag Beetle." Matt Summer. <http://maria.fremlin.de/stagbeetles/usa/lelaphus.html>

"Goliathus goliatus." BugzUK. <https://www.bugzuk.com/insects/beetles/goliathus-goliatus>

Hadley, Debbie. "How to Control Japanese Beetles." Thought Co. <https://www.thoughtco.com/how-to-control-japanese-beetles-1968381>

Harmon, Katherine. "World's Strongest Animal Effectively Benches 1,000 Times Its Body Weight." Scientific American. <https://blogs.scientificamerican.com/observations/worlds-strongest-animal-effectively-benches-1000-times-its-body-weight/>

"Hercules Beetle." A-Z Animals. <https://a-z-animals.com/animals/hercules-beetle/>

"Hercules Beetle." Animals.net. <https://a-z-animals.com/animals/hercules-beetle/>

"How to Get Rid of Fruit Flies." The Balance. <https://www.thebalance.com/get-rid-of-fruit-flies-1388144>

"How to Take Care of Stag Beetles (Kuwagata Mushi). Wander Tokyo. <http://wandertokyo.com/stag-beetle/>

Huger, Alois. "A Virus Disease of the Indian Rhinoceros Beetle, Oryctes rhinoceros (linnaeus), Caused by a New Type of Insect Virus Rhabdionvirus oryctes gen." *Journal of Invertebrate Pathology.* March 1966; 8(1): 38-51. <http://www.sciencedirect.com/science/article/pii/0022201166901017>

Inglese, Frank. "A Look into the Strange World of Japanese Beetle Fighting." Snap Thirty. <https://snapthirty.com/2016/04/12/a-look-into-the-strange-world-of-japanese-beetle-fighting/>

"Insects and Mites." USDA APHIS. <https://www.aphis.usda.gov/aphis/ourfocus/planthealth/import-information/permits/regulated-organism-and-soil-permits/insects-and-mites/CT_Insects>

"Japanese Rhinoceros Beetles (Allomyrina dichotoma)." TKS Science. <http://abrowntks.weebly.com/japanese-rhinoceros-beetles.html>

Kahler, Phil. "Raising Stag Beetles in the Classroom." TVJA.org. <http://www.tvja.org/science/pdf Documents/Invertebrates_Magazine_Mar-2011-Stag_Beetles.pdf>

Kasahara, Yasuhiko. "The Breeding/Rearing of *Dynastes hercules hercules*." Natural Worlds. <http://www.naturalworlds.org/scarabaeidae/manual/hercules/Dynastes_hercules_breeding_1.htm>

"Life Cycle of a Rhino Beetle." Science 6 Rhinoceros Beetle. <https://science6brhinocerosbeetle.weebly.com/life-cycle.html>

"Listed Vertebrate Animals." U.S. Fish and Wildlife Service. <https://ecos.fws.gov/ecp0/reports/ad-hoc-species-report?kingdom=I&status=E&status=T&status=EmE&status=EmT&status=SAE&status=SAT&mapstatus=1&fleadreg=on&fstatus=on&finvpop=on&header=Listed+Invertebrate+Animals>

Malory, Marcia. "Study Shows Rhinoceros Beetle Horns Evolved to Accommodate Species-Specific Fighting Styles." Phys.org. <https://phys.org/news/2014-09-rhinoceros-beetle-horns-evolved-accommodate.html>

Marschall, K.J. "Introduction of a New Virus Disease of the Coconut Rhinoceros Beetle in Western Samoa." Nature Publishing Group. <http://www.nature.com/nature/journal/v225/n5229/abs/225288a0.html?foxtrotcallback=true>

"*Megasoma elephas elephas* Breeding Report (Care Sheet)." Beetles as Pets. <http://beetlesaspets.blogspot.com/2016/03/megasoma-elephas-elephas-breeding.html>

Meier, Karl. "The Breeding/Rearing of Goliathus." Natural Worlds. <http://www.naturalworlds.org/goliathus/manual/Goliathus_breeding_1.htm>

Oder, Tom. "What Are Nematodes?" Mother Nature Network. <https://www.mnn.com/your-home/organic-farming-gardening/stories/what-are-nematodes>

"Paenibacillus popilliae." Cornell University College of Agriculture and Life Sciences. <https://biocontrol.entomology.cornell.edu/pathogens/paenibacillus.php>

Pappas, Stephanie. "How the Rhinoceros Beetle Got Its Horns." Live Science. <https://www.livescience.com/27851-rhinoceros-beetle-horn-evolution.html>

"Pest Beetle Control with Natural Solutions." Arbico Organics. <http://www.arbico-organics.com/category/pest-solver-guide-beetles>

"Rhino Beetle Care." P&K Pets. <http://www.pkpets.com.au/images/pdf-care-list/Info%20Sheet%2020%20-%20Rhino%20Beetle.pdf>

"Rhino Beetle Care Sheet." Bugs in Cyberspace. <http://www.bugsincyberspace.com/Rhino_Beetle_Care_Sheet.html>

"Rhinoceros Beetle." Animal Corner. <https://animalcorner.co.uk/animals/rhinoceros-beetle/>

"Subfamily Lucanini." BugGuide. <http://bugguide.net/node/view/558921/bgpage>

"The European Rhinoceros Beetle." Beetles as Pets. <http://beetlesaspets.blogspot.com/2014/01/the-european-rhinoceros-beetle-oryctes.html>

"The Rhino Beetle Life Cycle." RhinoBeetle.co.uk. <https://www.rhinobeetle.co.uk/index.php/template/rhinobeetle-lifecycle>

Tiago, Patricia Vieira. "Biological Insect Control Using Metarhizium anisopliae: Morphological, Molecular, and Ecological Aspects." Sci ELO. <http://www.scielo.br/scielo.php?script=sci_arttext&pid=S0103-84782014000400012>

Vinje, E. "Bacillus thuringiensis Products." Planet Natural Research Center. <https://www.planetnatural.com/bacillus-thuringiensis/>

Wallin, Bill. "Hercules Beetles." University of Kentucky Entomology. <http://www.uky.edu/Ag/CritterFiles/casefile/insects/beetles/hercules/rearing/rearing.htm>

"What Kind of Illnesses Do Insects Get? Do We Have the Medical Knowledge to Cure an Insect if We Knew It Was Sick?" Scientific American. <https://www.scientificamerican.com/article/what-kind-of-illnesses-do/>

Yong, Ed. "Rhino Beetle Weapons Match their Fighting Styles." National Geographic. <http://phenomena.nationalgeographic.com/2014/09/09/rhino-beetle-weapons-match-their-fighting-styles/>

Image Credits

Page 2 – Pixabay user Kalmankovats <https://pixabay.com/en/animal-bug-natur-green-brown-male-2105998/>

Page 8 – Pixabay user ralflin <https://pixabay.com/en/rhinoceros-beetle-errors-insect-828323/>

Page 17 – Wikimedia Commons <https://commons.wikimedia.org/wiki/File:Hercules.beetle.arp.jpg>

Page 22 – Wikimedia Commons <https://commons.wikimedia.org/wiki/Megasoma_elephas#/media/File:Elephant_Beetle_Megasoma_elephas_Male_Side_2699px.jpg>

Page 25 – Wikimedia Commons <https://commons.wikimedia.org/wiki/File:Kabutomushi-20070710.jpg>

Page 27 – Wikimedia Commons <https://commons.wikimedia.org/wiki/File:Oryctes_nasicornis_Thailand.jpg>

Page 58 – Wikimedia Commons <https://commons.wikimedia.org/wiki/File:Hercules_beetle_(Dynastes_hercules)_-_24_July_2010.jpg>

Page 65 – Pixabay user Leechentou <https://pixabay.com/en/stag-beetle-beetle-war-anti-host-830371/>

Page 71 – Wikimedia Commons <https://commons.wikimedia.org/wiki/File:Scarabaeidae_-_Goliathus_goliatus.JPG>

Printed in Great Britain
by Amazon